MW00977190

Show Your Love

Jasmine L. Cummings

Copyright © 2012 Jasmine L. Cummings

All rights reserved.

ISBN-10:   1470022907

ISBN-13: 978-1470022907

DEDICATION

This book is dedicated to my mother,
Barbara D. Haynes, my first teacher about life,
Who showed me that it is more important to SHOW your love,
than to just say the words.

CONTENTS

ACKNOWLEDGMENTS

I would like to thank those that gave me the encouragement I needed to Take Out My Pen to Write. God, who continues to be my source of inspiration, My mother and father, the late James L. Haynes, and the late Barbara D. Grant-Haynes, Dr. Maya Angelou, MY American Idol, Irma Long, a Chicago Teacher that gave me my first blank book, (It took a while, but I filled it with words.) my children: Darien, Jazia and JaZiya, who share my love of creativity,

Thanks for knowing when I needed to be alone with my thoughts.

Lula, for listening to the poems, and critiquing them before anyone else saw them.

Teddy, Curtis, Bennye J, Ervin, Pam, Richard, and the many others that helped make my dreams, my realities.

1~ SHOW YOUR LOVE

Show your love by what you do,
and not by what you say.
That's how one will know it's true,
it's the only way.
Don't tell me that you hold me dear,
and when I need you
you're not here.
Don't say I know how you feel about me,
I only go by what I see.
I don't need one who talks the talk;
give me one who
walks the walk.
If your love is truly real,
don't just say it,
make me feel.

2~ A BOND OF LOVE

A bond of love that has lasted for years,
through the success, disappointments, heartbreak and tears.
A bond unspoken---no need for it to be,
to know that this person would always be there for me.
A bond of strength that has kept me strong.
The awareness of this, helps me to get along.
A bond unbroken, and this I know is true,
because I will always be there, and he's been right there too.
A bond of friendship, that will bind us to the end--
I'm so glad that I will always call this person my friend.

3~ YOU ARE THE MAN

You are the man, the only man,
That really makes me smile.
For me to realize this fact,
Took much more than a while.
Just when my life had gotten
Just as down as it could be,
In you came to light the flame
that burns inside of me.
I'll never really know
just what powers you possess,
All I can tell is it's a spell
my heart has done the rest.
You bring out every side of me
and this I know is true:
You're all the man
I'll ever need,
And I'm the only woman for you.

4~ AND THEN CAME YOU

My days were dark and lonely too, without spark-
And then came you.
No one could have told me so
I was clueless - Now, I know.
You've made my life a beautiful song.
How did I know you'd come along?
To brighten up my sunless days,
To make me happy, in so many ways.
In my mind, this feels so right,
And my dreams ARE so much sweeter at night.
True feelings like this I never knew, my life was missing-
And then came you.

5~WHAT IS LOVE?

Love is as simple as two children promising to be friends.

Love is as complicated as a man and a woman vowing their love will never end.

Love is as beautiful as staring into a lover's eyes by candlelight,

But when it's a mere obsession, and just a possession,

It breeds misery, and it bites.

Love is being patient, when you don't like to wait,

Love is talking, as well as LISTENING to your chosen mate.

Love is holding your tongue, even when you know you're right,

Love always seeks peace, and avoids a fight.

Love is a sacrifice. Putting your wants on hold,

Believing that because you did, you would have joy a thousand fold.

Love is looking at your child and saying, "Whatever he is, he's mine".

Love is looking at your man and saying, "That guy STILL looks fine".

Love is not saying, "Be there for me, and I'll be there for you",

Love is saying, "I'll be here ALWAYS, and I hope you'll be here too".

Love is trust and certainty, that doesn't leave you in doubt.

Love ignites an eternal flame that can never, ever, die out.

Love is as genuine, as Jesus dying on the cross.

Love is something we all must have no matter what the cost.

6~ Are You in Love, or Are You Crazy?

Many people love you, say so, and mean it.
Others say they love you, and really don't mean it.
How do you know who's telling the truth?
The answer is simple.
Those that really love you, don't have to say it,
But show it. This is the only way that you'd really
Know it.
Real love, to me, is craziness.
If I say I love you, I mean there is something about you
That I like a lot.
It could be your smile at the right time each day,
It could even be the words of encouragement that you say.
It could be a special thing that you know how to do, it could be
Your perseverance or your strength too.
If I say I'm crazy about you, I mean that I think about you
Constantly.
If you're not around, I wonder where you are.
If I'm shopping, I'm thinking of something that you
Might like.
If I'm alone, I'm thinking of things like this to write
I'm crazy about you.

7~WHAT COULD HAVE BEEN

It could have been this,
it should have been that,
I could have done more,
instead of just sat.
I should have gone slow,
when I wanted things fast,
I should have taken more time,
to make the good things last.
I should have gone out,
when I stayed inside,
I should have laughed,
the times I've cried.
It could have been you,
instead of him,
life should be more planned,
instead of more whim.
There are so many things
that I could have done,
But if I can't please myself,
I can please no one.

8~WITHOUT QUESTION

I am entrusting you with my love,
without question.
I have no qualms about allowing you
To feel how my heart beats when you're
Near me,
without question.
I've let you become more familiar
with my true soul, as I have no other
without question.
I've lain before you baring my heart
totally allowing you view every one of the
Scars, bumps, and bruises of my life
both inner and outer.
without question.
All these things I do, when I give myself
to you.
You accept me without question,
And without question,
I love you.

9~LOVE WILL SAVE THE DAY

Love WILL save the day.
The love of those that care
how my story unfolds.
The love of those that write the books
that help tell me that a way
CAN be made out of no way,
and prove that I am truly
the only author
of the only dictionary
that defines ME.
The love of self that gives me
the determination to rise
whenever I fall.
The love of those that assist me
in making my dreams, my realities.
YES!--- Love WILL save,
not only the day,
but my lifetime as well.

10~SOFTLY INTO MY MORNING

Softly into my morning,
you stepped out of my dream.
A beautiful day is dawning,
and that's what you make it seem.
WHATEVER I had planned for today,
is going on hold for now,
because I want to spend each moment with you,
Today, ALL day, somehow.
And when the day is over,
I know ALL will be so right.
For Just as softly as into MY morning you came,
I will creep softly into YOUR good night.

11~IF I HAVE NEVER TOLD YOU

If I have never told you,
you've made my life sublime.
It must be the way,
you've brightened my day,
each and every time.
If I have never told you,
You've made my life complete.
From the day you've entered it,
You managed to center it.
That being QUITE the feat.
If I have never told you,
I'm really proud of you.
You're my treasure, my pride,
you touch feelings deep inside,
with the many things that you do.
If I have never told you,
you've impressed me more than
just a bit.
And although the words may,
have been hard for ME to say,
I just wanted to let YOU know it.

12~IF I HAD MET YOU SOONER

If I had met you sooner,

I never would have made

the mistakes I made before,

not knowing how life was played.

If I had met you before,

I never would have paid

such high a cost for loving,

leaving my life in disarray.

But now I know just who I love,

and although wiser, I'm new to love.

I feel we'll make it through my love;

you are for whom I've prayed.

13~I TAKE OUT MY PEN TO WRITE

Thoughts and words take on a blurry view,
As I collect myself , to write a poem for you.
I think of the dream I had last night,
But no, that's TOO steamy. That isn't right.
I think of words, used to describe you,
But now it seems as though,
Those words won't do.
But yet...I take out my pen to write.
To the one I adore, each day I love you more,
For you light up every corner of my world.
Your love sends me reeling, and I get the feeling,
That I must be the luckiest girl.
Each and every day, I hope and pray,
In MY arms you'll ever be.
Each and every night, my mind takes this flight...
And STILL it's only YOU I see.
But YET...I take out my pen to write.

14~A MOTHER'S LOVE

A mother's love is like no other,
for nothing can replace,
one whose been by your side from day one,
and can always bring a smile to your face.
She's been right there from the beginning,
to comfort you when you've cried.
She was your first teacher about life,
and just seemed to know how you felt inside.
Her cheers are the loudest when you win,
she gives you the most consolation when you fall.
When you add it all up, you just must confess
that she's the best friend of them all.
Always there to help with anything,
always there with that needed shove,
and with kids of your own, you'll do the same,
because MOTHER is synonymous with LOVE.

15~GOODNIGHT MY PRINCE

As nighttime falls, and you're in your bed,
I hope a lovely dream fills your head.
One fond thought--you'll smile when you see,
that you are loved more than any man could be.
Goodnight my Prince,
And as you dream, as you recall how hard a day it may have seemed,
Remember—heavy is the head which wears the crown,
You can't just take it off, nor can you put it down.
Goodnight my Prince,
and upon your wake, on the very first utterance or word you make,
May you give thanks to the Lord above,
for filling your world with so much love.

16~THE KING WITHOUT A CROWN

The King without a crown,

never let his people down,

but tried to get us ALL to a higher place.

Unstoppable he seemed,

led only by his dream,

he taught us it's NEVER right to divide our world by race.

He wanted us to set our minds,

to a BETTER place and time,

and showed us that all we have to do is dream.

When we let his dream abound,

The world is better all around.

It's a better place because of a man called Dr. King.

17~THE ONE AND ONLY MS.PATTI LABELLE

The Beautiful is who you are,
And that title, SO fits YOU.
For it not only says WHAT you are,
It tells the WAY you DO, what you DO.
Many times, your name did not match—
What LIFE had in store for you,
But because your nature is to live life beautifully,
You OVERCAME those obstacles too.
Your beauty, both inner AND outer,
Shines through, in what you DO so well,
Timeless beauty by far,
You most CERTAINLY ARE,
The One and ONLY---

Ms. Patti LaBelle!

18~THE DAY I MET DR. MAYA ANGELOU

The day I met you, Dr. Angelou,
It made me realize,
That the woman who had inspired me~
was right before my eyes!
It didn't matter that I was at the end of the line,
and the line was extremely long,
For I was going to meet a truly beautiful mind, so nothing to me,
could go wrong.
I endured the wait by wondering, "What things would I say to
her?"
But I was amazed when I stood before you, and my thoughts were
in a blur.
I had so much I wanted to tell you,
though I knew you didn't have the time,
I wanted you to know that you had inspired me,
to write my own verse and rime.
I wanted to show you my works,
and discuss technique in depth.
But you had a long day, and it was late.
There was just no time left.
Someday I'm sure we'll meet again, perhaps that can be arranged.
Because meeting you was the fulfillment of my dream,

21

And here's a poem for YOU for a change.

19~I'LL THINK ABOUT THE GOOD TIMES MICHAEL

I'll think about the good times,
For in my mind, they're set.
The J5 days, your smile, your ways, I can NEVER forget.
I'll think about the good times, as you find your corner of the sky,
The songs that made us feel so happy, the songs that made us cry.
Remember the times you broke out in dance,
The times you broke out in song,
Your style, your grace, rests in a peaceful place,
There just ain't no sunshine, since YOU'VE been gone.
You knew we were, "THE WORLD" ,
at times this world made you want to Scream, "Leave me alone,"
"give me space", let's make this world a BETTER place,
With a child's heart, gone too soon, it seemed.
Thank you for being such a THRILLER! And that's what you will
continue to be,
For now, and forever more, you've left the world our LEGACY.
*May you finally rest in peace.

20~BLACK IS MORE THAN JUST A COLOR

Black is more than just a color; it's a proud way of life.
To be a Black American, is representing our successes through our strife.
All of those great people, who have shown us the right way,
Have unlocked many of the doors, that we walk through today.
Thousands of years ago, when Pharaoh had us bound,
MOSES led us to the promised land where freedom could be found.
Hundreds of years later, when we were enslaved again,
Harriet Tubman led the way, on a railroad without a train.
Many of years after, Abe Lincoln set us free,
A king without a crown led the way,
when people we weren't considered to be.
So I wear my color proudly, and I carry the torch with pride.
For I represent a race, whose history NO man can hide.

21~WE AS A PEOPLE, WILL GET TO THE PROMISED LAND

Like Moses, being faced with the Red Sea in front of him, and
Pharaoh's army behind him, the Lord made a way out of no way,
for him to lead his people to the promised land.
Like Harriet Tubman, led hundreds of slaves to freedom,
by way of the underground railroad---NORTH---to the promised
land,
knowing that with a high price on her head,
her life, and the lives of those she led, were threatened with each
and every trip.
Like Dr. Martin Luther King Jr., armed only with his dream for a
better world,
Marched right through the worst kind of hatred.
-The hard rock of racism.
He faced, segregation, jail, the KKK, and death, HEAD ON!
Peacefully changing our lives forever!
We, as a people, have come a long way,
and, we-as a people, have a long way to go,
But we-as a people, will get there, to that Promised Land.

22~THE DREAM

On wings, like eagles, we fly.
Hope of yesterday's tomorrow sky.
Old ways to fade away.
The dream is realized today.
Real hope reigns through and through,
The world sees what a people can do.
No longer are things the same.
The dream is ours to claim.
A feeling so deep inside,
One that can only be known
as pride.
Long suffrage behind in our past.
The dream is ours at last!
Oh SAY! Did you EVER see?
My country, tis really of THEE!
Now let freedom reign,
Lift your voices and sing,
AMERICA the DREAM is ME!

23~PERPETUAL STORM

My love for you is like a Perpetual Storm.

I thought it strange at first, but it feels so like the norm.

It twists, tosses, and rages, tearing through my very core.

Yet while going through these stages, I love you even more.

Poems written and published by:

Jasmine L. Cummings

classyjazzcreations@yahoo.com
Copyright ©2012 Jasmine Lynetta Cummings

ABOUT THE AUTHOR

Jasmine L. Cummings, born and raised in Chicago, IL. , is a
Chicago Poet. "As a child, I attended The American Conservatory
of Music, as my family was totally immersed in the fine arts, and I
have been singing since I could talk. I have always wanted to write
music, but that shifted to a love of writing poetry. I attended Carver
Area High School, where I honed my vocal skills with the
Madrigals under the direction of Ms. Bennye J. Tharp.
My songwriting and instrumental skills under the direction of my
mother, Barbara D. Haynes, who wrote music , taught herself to
play the piano and had one of her songs, And He Cares, recorded
by Sam Cooke and The Soul Stirrers on the SARS record label.
My father, James L. Haynes diligently took me to extra classes in
Music and French."
After graduation, she studied at DePaul University in Chicago,
where she was a member of DePaul's Gospel Choir . "I have spent
the past 26 years working for the Chicago Public Schools as a
teacher, and have taught hundreds of students to sing in perfect
harmony."

"These poems were written during my lifetime as a teacher. They are passionate, and they recall tenderness and pain. They have a rare sanity which reaches the mind as well as the heart."

"Years ago at DePaul, a professor once told me: "What doesn't come from the heart, will never reach a heart." I've never forgotten what he said that day, and I've applied it to my life both in teaching and in my writing."

"It is my hope that each poem reaches your heart, because each one came from mine."

~Jasmine L. Cummings

Afterthoughts:

If it were not for those that hoped I'd fall,
I might have never climbed the wall,
That got me to the other side.
My afterthought today is, Pride.

~Jazz

Made in the USA
Columbia, SC
05 October 2022

68812115R00022